Poetry
Is

Poetry Is

By

Brian T. Ballotta

To Shanai, for all your love and support, you opened my eyes to many things. And to Zach, Alyssa, Anna, Haley, Mary, and Aubrey, Don't ever give up on your dreams, they do come true...

Table of Contents

III.   *Through These Eyes*

IV.   *Discovery*

V.   New Beginnings

VI.   *Lessons Learned*

Poetry is many things to many people. It is a release from the daily stresses of life, a security blanket, a way to communicate, even a way to tell the tale of our life. Poetry can be the flight of a butterfly, the bark of a dog, the roar of an engine, or the flight of a baseball off of a bat. Poetry can be a heartbeat of a loved one or a streak of lightning across the sky. To me poetry has become an outlet. It is a glimpse at the path I've traveled through the stages of life.

These stages come and go with the blink of an eye. Some of us grow in leaps and bounds. Some grow in bursts and lulls. And still some grow in a steady and gradual climb. Some of us move through these stages in a combination of the three. The best part of this process is being able to share it with those around you. Our first steps, first words, first time behind the wheel, are all magical moments. The events at the time may not seem so; whether it is a breakup, loss of someone dear, a tragic accident; but remembering the friends that helped us through brings a smile to our faces. We don't remember all of the steps we take, but they leave a lasting impression.

Through these events we grow, learning many things. We learn about the world around us, both large and small. Most importantly we learn about ourselves; who we are, and what we believe. We find our way one step at a time, building with every stride. Over the years we grow, change for better and for worse. It's not the situations in life, but what we take from them that is important.

I
Humble Beginnings...

"Impressions"

From the day I met you

You stole my heart

I will never forget you

If I am smart

My friend you are

My devotion will not bend

When you move away so far

Our friendship will not end

"Locked Away"

My heart is a hidden treasure chest
Full of love and glee
It will not rest
Until I find
The one who holds the key
There is gold
Locked inside of it
Or so I am told
By those
Who've seen it
It holds great worth
That which is inside
To one on this earth
Whoever she is
That chooses to hide

"Searching for..."

I am so alone
Down to the bone
I feel so much
But without a touch
I cannot give
And I cannot live
The only way
I can say
To free my heart
Is with this art
Oh can there be
Another way to set me free

"Do You See?"

Do you see
Or is it just me
The pain I'm in
You always could help me win
The pain is great
And so is the hate
That is shown to me
By all those you see
There are a few points of light
But they are so bright
And you are one
That's as bright as the sun
You can bring me glee
When I want to flee
You keep me sane
And show me much to gain
When I shed a tear
You show me there is nothing to fear
When someone broke my heart
And I fell apart
You could put me together
And mend me forever
What you can do
Is unknown to you
I wasn't so sure
Of my feelings so pure
To let you see
What you mean to me

"Long Time Friends"

Our friendship is long

It has made me strong

To pull us apart

Would break my heart

You made things bright

When they were such a fright

"Dedication"

You are so sweet
You are so fair
Your voice is a treat
You have beautiful hair
When you are gone
It will be hard
But I will go on
Our friendship I will guard
Till the end of time
As I make a beautiful rhyme

"You"

Your smile is bright
Your mind is so open
You make things right
Even when I'm heartbroken

You open up my soul
You lighten my heart
You have a big role
So you must be smart

"When you need..."

When there is rain
Or there is pain
I'll be there for you
All the way through
When it is cold
Or you need someone to hold
I'll be there
No matter when or where
When there is fear
Or you need someone to hear
I'll give my all
To stop the fall
When all seems hopeless
And you are restless
I will put to the test
And do my best
To brighten your day
In every way

"Frustrating Decisions"

I am so full of confusion
I don't know who to choose
I am full of frustration
Because I don't want to lose
Anyone as part of my life
They are all so sweet
And put up with me thru all my strife
Their love is a treat
It opens my heart
But who will get the treasure
Who is that smart
To allow me to show her pleasure

"Steps To Peace"

I am so dazed
But none know I'm fazed
The noise is so loud
It's like I'm on a cloud
The room is dark
Yet I see a spark
It starts very dim
Down at the rim
It then grew
This is true
Then it was bright
Yes that is right
I see a way out
So I no longer doubt

II
Pain, Mistakes, and Love

12-5-96

I made a mistake
In what I said
Now I stay awake
While I lie here in bed
This day was not good
As you have seen
So I hope you understand
What I said I did mean
You mean so much
That my inside went bust
When I spoke as such
And me you didn't trust

"You Are..."

When I see you everyday
I feel good in every way
You are wise and very smart
You have an open mind and giant heart
You're always there in my time of need
So I thought I'd give you this to read
Your smile is so big and bright
It makes my soul so strong and light
Now I hope that you can see
What your friendship means to me
Just let me know
The way to go
If there is anything you need me do
I would be honored to do anything for you
You always find a way to make me smile
Not for a minute but for a while

"No Way Out"

My world is torture
My life is hell
As for the future
I cannot tell
There is not much
That I can see
To do like such
To save me
I see so few
And no way out
I wish I knew
What this is about
I could die
But leave too much undone
So that is why
That is not the one
I could kill
And get a loud yelp
I do have the will
But that will not help

"Life's Twist"

My life took a twist
So I made a list
Of things undone
I have not done one
I do not know
Who I will show
The pressure to fight
To make things right
Is too strong
And been on me too long

"All Wrong"

My heart is dyin'
My soul is cryin'
My world is breakin'
My ground is shakin'
I could be flyin'
But there's no point in tryin'
I try wakin'
But my strength is taken
Loved one's dyin'
Best friends lyin'
Don't know what to do
Or who to run to
Things fall apart
And I'm not very smart
Or talented enough
To survive the rough
And to make it stop
So I end up on top

"Idea"

I heard an idea
That was so nice
I said yeah
To add some spice
The sweet whipped cream
And the nice soft skin
Made it sound like a dream
But actually is a sin
I was told about chocolate sauce
To my delight
I was left at a loss
That made my night
To watch in the shower
Can arouse anyone's passion
To see such a flower
In such sweet action

"Potential"

There is so much
That I can see
And to touch
That's out there for me
It gives me strength
To live and go on
For a great length
And not be gone
Like a horse trottin'
In a field by himself
I've been forgotten
And put on the shelf

"Wrong Words"

I made a mistake
And spoke again
I can't catch a break
Even if I use my brain
When I do think
And try to change my ways
I get right to the brink
But I just can't beat the craze
I always hit a wall
When I try to change
I start to fall
And feel really strange
I begin to feel weak
As time passes by
I didn't reach the peak
But I don't know why

"Unsure Hope"

Things seem strange
It feels kinda nice
That things could change
But it makes me think twice
I wish it were true
About a someone
And how she feels
So I would not be blue
It would make me run
Right to her side
To show her fun
And show me not to hide
It would make my heart so light
And make my mind so clear
If I had her to hold tight
And say the words she wants to hear

"Shaken Confidence"

I see one bright spot
Who knows not who she is
It ties me in a knot
And confuses me, all this
I don't know what to say
For she may like another
In the same way
So I question and wonder
Why even try
With words so kind
Because I do not cry
With her on my mind
Life seems so easy
And days seem so fair
When it becomes breezy
And her scent is in the air
It is so sweet
As my nose, it passes under
My heart begins to beat
Like the sound of thunder

"Stolen Happiness"

I feel so flushed
Yet am so full
I haven't been crushed
But it feels like bull
I have nowhere to go
To find any escapes
I have nothing to show
Except for some scrapes
I thought I found one
To show me a way out
But that dream was undone
Not that there was doubt
Why should things go right
That would be good
Why should days be bright
Is there a reason they would

"Beauty Begets Evil"

I see you there
Your beauty astounds
I know not why or where
But my heart pounds
I would no longer be under
If I knew why
But I tremble like thunder
Trying not to cry
I have a blank stare
About my face
No one seems to care
Not even a trace
I see a great cliff
Off which to leap
When and if
I see one more creep

"Magical?"

There is a magical night
That I may never see
It would go from dark to light
With or without me
There is a chance I may see it
Though that chance is slim
If you look just a bit
Things seem quite grim
Although things are dark
And slightly blurry
There may be a spark
To start such a flurry
That can change things around
And cause me to jump
And also astound
While creating a thump

"Room of Passion"

As I open my eyes
I see a great beauty
On silk laden bed she lies
To pleasure her is my duty
A room full of roses
Petals on the bed
As the door closes
On a background of red
There is a sweet scent
Lingering in the room
Such time and money spent
To make an idea bloom
A full body massage
A hot sponge bath with sweet oils
All seems like a mirage
But will remove all your toils

"Picked Apart"

I give you my heart
Because I am sure
And you pick it apart
Like my love is not pure
You throw it in my face
And laugh at me
As I give chase
To let you see
I would do anything for you
And you know not why
There are things I would do
Such as give up and die
I show you an opening
And you don't care
You may be listening
But you have a blank stare

"Soothing Touch"

The water is drawn
The petals I add
To please until dawn
This lady who is sad
I caress her gently
From head to toe
Until it is apparently
Time to go
I wish not to depart
While she's in her present state
Though I must brighten her heart
On another date
Every time she sighs
It's a call to me
So when she opens her eyes
It's I she'll see
To pleasure her in every way
To fill her every want and need
From now on, every day
As long as I can lead

"Beauty's Charm"

I lay her down
And give her a kiss
She deserves a crown
And a life of bliss
Her beautiful hair
And wonderful eyes
Lighten the air
And wipe out all lies
I would shower her with roses
As she lies on the silk
After the door closes
Her skin feels like silk
Her lips taste so sweet
Just like honey
Her voice is a treat
That you can't buy with money

"Sweet Flavors"

Her skin is so soft
Her lips are so sweet
Up in the loft
There is such a treat
There are sweet strawberries
In a bowl by the bed
Also with cherries
In such deep tones of red
The fruit crosses her lips
With juices so mild
She gets sent on long trips
By the taste of fruit so wild
I will fulfill her every dream
And look at her face
When I bring whipped cream
To her lying on silk and lace

"Broken Pledge"

She found her way out
But it just wasn't right
Now there's no doubt
That I will fight
I was on edge
And he gave a shove
By breaking the pledge
He made to love
He deserves to die
Probably by my hand
He will cry
When my fist lands
He lost all face
And he, I should pound
To leave not a trace
Of a body six feet underground

"Untitled"

Your lips are sweet
Like sugar and honey
Your voice is a treat
Not buyable with money
You bring a spark
To a room
That is dark
And wipe away gloom

"Silent Torment"

My hands are tied
Through no fault of my own
Harder I'd have tried
If I had only known
I wish I could take you away
And show you better things
But you'd rather stay
And see what time brings
My heart I am giving
But it, you don't want
So I go on living
As your friend and confidante
You say I care differently
Which I see as true
So I wait patiently
To show you I do
The question I ask
Is "did he really care?"
Or was it a mask
Over feelings so bare
I know you fear
Being single and alone
But I'll be here
In person or on the phone
To me you're the world
You make things better in every way
In a ball I'm curled
Not knowing if you're ok
For I'd do anything
Even if I had to die
'Cause to me you mean everything
And that is no lie

"Holding Strong"

I am never lost
When you are near
There is no cost
I have nothing to fear
If I were to lose you
And this is no lie
I wouldn't know what to do
And would probably die
You mean too much
To see you treated like dirt
I wish I could touch
And wipe away the hurt
I want to take your pain
And make you smile
Shelter you from the rain
For quite a while
I don't know where to begin
Or where it will end
I just want to let you in
And show my feelings will not bend

"Blind Eye"

The color of your eyes
Is a sweet blue
Like the sunny skies
Which I see in you

You need to be so free
But now you want out
And as far as I can see
There is still a doubt

I know you see the facts
And don't want to believe it
So you put on acts
And it's taking all your wit

"Daily Torment"

You treat me like shit
You say it's on me
But it's not me one bit
Oh why can't you see

I didn't do a thing
Yet you say I do
Why should I hang and swing
When it's all because of you

You say it's not
But you don't know
Maybe some but not a lot
And I don't show

Because that's what I choose
You think you know what I need
That idea you should lose
Because no one does it feed

You take what is mine
Just on a whim
Like some kind of fine
Or taking a limb

I need to be left alone
I need my freedom
I need to set my own tone
I need not to feel dumb

"What I've done"

Some things were said
Between us last night
So I lie here in bed
And think what I might

It left me in shock
And with a question
Or two you may mock
So them I do not mention

I want to ask
But I know not if I should
It is a hard task
Even if I could

I don't want to lose you
Because of anything I've done
I wish I knew what to do
To make my mistakes none

I know it's a surprise
And I don't know why
I wasn't sure it was wise
But I had to try

"Hope and Joy"

I see a glimmer of hope
It's a good start
And I would be a dope
Not to give it my whole heart

I wish I knew
When things go my way
What I had to do
To get them to stay

Things are going good
At least they look
As best as they could
From the turn life took

If given the chance
The time I would cherish
Like the big dance
I hope wouldn't perish

"Eased Troubles"

Your skin is soft to the touch
Your voice is sweet to the ear
I have never felt so much
As when you are near

I wish you could stay forever
But all I get is a glance
And think I will never
Get such a chance

Your touch is gentle
And makes me relax
You make me sentimental
And my energy you don't tax

You make all my troubles
Fly away so distant
My energy doubles
In one short instant

I feel invisible
When you're around
You are irresistible
Your beauty astounds

"Lies Form Chains"

You could be free
But you won't do
As far as I can see
What you need to

I know it's hard
To do this deed
But you hold the card
And this is all you need

I will be here for you
To shelter you from the rain
And also to
Help you through the pain

You know how you felt
And he can talk
So either you melt
Or you turn and walk

You've been treated like dirt
Instead of a gem
There's been too much hurt
So just get rid of them

"Sweetest Dreams"

Sweet dreams
Are made of thee
But this it seems
You cannot see

I have no chance
Or it's so small
Or I'm in a trance
And will miss my call

If there's more I can do
To gain your heart
I would do it for you
Like a work of art

I see your love
As so soft and bright
Just like a dove
So pure and white

I wish I could have a piece
And give you the same
With hope it will never cease
If my way it ever came

"Calming the Beast"

Few tears run down my cheek
Though I don't often find
What it is I seek
As if I was totally blind

I find this strength
In one and only
And at length
You make me not lonely

You make me timid
With your soft touch
When I am amid
Conditions as such

Your sweet song
Is to my ears a feast
It didn't take you long
To soothe this savage beast

You wipe away pain
And bring on good thought
Don't run from the rain
Is what I am taught

"Searching For Your King"

You are a queen
And deserve a good king
But from what I've seen
You still need this thing

The queen you are
Is of the heart
Wishing on a star
For someone that smart

You like your love served
On a silver platter
And what you deserve
To me does matter

You deserve all the best
To see you suffer is wrong
So put all to the test
And it will not be long

"The Moon"

I can't decide
Which way to go
I can't hide
This much I know

There is more than one way
For me to travel
It will take more than a day
For me to unravel

I am confused
And don't know where to turn
I have not been refused
But there is a lot I must learn

It will not be soon
But I hope I may see
If reaching for the moon
Is really meant to be

"The Rose"

The rose was a gift
From me to you
In hope that it would lift
Your hopes and happiness too

You are so deserving
Of a gift so sweet
To him it was unnerving
But for you it was a treat

You will receive more
And nothing will compare
Of this I am sure
To the beauty both share

"Do I Say?"

I don't know how to explain
How I feel inside
As I sit here in the rain
I just cannot decide

I care more than you know
Or maybe you do see
But it is hard to show
Not knowing if it could be

I would like a shot
To maybe show you
What I've got
And what I'll do

I don't want to lose
What we have here
It's up to you to choose
But that is what I fear

The choice is yours
To consider and make
To open the doors
And what is behind them take

Just please don't take away
What you've already given
I would not know what to say
And wouldn't know how to go on livin'

"In My Mind"

I am deep in thought
Cold and shaking
I feel like I've fought
And am slowly breaking

I don't know what to do
About the way I feel
I don't know how to tell you
I don't know if it's real

I have many questions to ask
But I don't know how to say
It will be a very large task
But I must get it out of the way

I want to be there
To lighten your heart
I don't know when, where
Or if it is my part

It would be great
If I could fill that space
But I don't know how I rate
Although that's the usual case

"Words"

I care for you
More than words can say
I guess words must do
I see no other way

I see you in my dreams
You are always on my mind
You bring out my best it seems
And you are always kind

I would give my all
If I were your man
I would answer your every call
As fast as I can

I've never felt this way before
It feels so good and so right
And I feel it more
When you are in my sight

"Dreams Come True"

I've seen a dream come true
I've always hoped and dreamed
Of being able to be with you
For some time, so far away it seemed

It is not a dream anymore
Now that you are here
You I can and do adore
And have only one thing to fear

The thought of your loss
Would leave a great void
That I could not cross
And I wish to avoid

No matter what gets in our way
I will do my best to help overcome
In hopes that with you I can stay
And my heart this comes from

When I feel your soft touch
I am never blue
I can relax so much
And I know I love you

"Could It Be"

I sit here and dream
To find what I can see
And for now it does seem
Like it could just be

In a short jump in time
It will feel maybe not
So I feel like a boxed in mime
With pressure high and temp so hot

I wish I knew
Which path to take
I wish I could view
The decision I should make

I want to tell you
Exactly how I feel
But I don't know what to do
To show you it is real

"Finding Happiness"

My dreams are sweet
My thoughts are glad
To think of you is a treat
I am no longer sad

Always I wish so much
To never leave your side
To always feel your touch
To take this magical ride

When I am near you
There are no worries in sight
And in most everything I do
It all seems to go right

The grass is so green
The sky is so blue
But nothing I have seen
Is as pretty as you

"Love's Power"

This is great power
This thing called love
It will never cower
And is pure as a dove

It has great strength
Shown in my tears
It goes to great length
To wipe away your fears

To know I can feel
With such great emotion
Is now oh so real
But was once just a notion

I wish I could see you to bed
And then to watch you rise
My love is fed
By what I see in your eyes

Its power is great
And happy I have been
Since I found my soul mate
In you I've seen

"Blissful Beauty"

I feel such bliss
When I hear your voice
You I would not miss
If I had my choice

To be with you always
Is such a great dream
To see you for the rest of my days
Is not as far away as it seems

The rose was a gift
For my sexy blue-eyed playboy bunny
And the spirit it did lift
Of both me and my honey

I love you so much
I hurt to see you upset
I wish that my touch
Would all bad reset

You make my world bright
You always change my mood
You make things so right
When the world is so rude

The rose's beauty doesn't compare
To the beauty of my baby
A beauty so rare
That so pretty no one else shall be

"Ode to a Friend"

Your friendship is grand
Like a large open land
Your smile is bright
It makes a day go right

Your love is true
And when you are blue
Here to help I will be
You can count on me

Patience is a must
And hope you do trust
That no matter what time
I will be there with a cheerful rhyme

You may be sad
And this is quite bad
So I will make you smile
Not for just a minute but a long while

"Dark Rain"

My heart you did capture
With your sweet voice
I am in rapture
I'm glad to get the choice

My love does immortalize
You in my life and death
Together we will rise
With each and every breath

My love will never fade
For that would cause great pain
Like an overwhelming raid
During a dark and evil rain

"Life's Challenges"

Life gets tough
There is great pain
It will always be rough
But there is shelter from the rain

I found my shelter
Deep in your heart
For some it is helter skelter
But for me it is a work of art

There may be hardships that we will see
But it shouldn't make the distance longer
That may be between you and me
It should make us stronger

The more we go through
The better we become
And of all the things we say and do
This is where our chance comes from

"Losing Touch"

I've lost too much
For me to bare
To neither see nor touch
This is not fair

You say leave you not
Yet you run from me
Now I'm in a spot
And I can't be free

Free from this pain
This wound is deep
It makes me insane
Out my love does seep

Please say what I did
To make this all start
Can I please make a bid
For a piece of your heart

Either as a bit
Or as a whole
If I know where I sit
I'll deal with the toll

III
Through These Eyes

"The Hard Way"

You turn from me
Visit with a liar
Can't you see
You're playing with fire

He'll steer you wrong
Because of what he knows
Your will isn't strong
And yes this does show

He'll play to your weakness
He'll toy with your mind
He lives on his sleekness
Your heart he will bind

You won't know what to do
You won't know where to turn
He'll turn around and hurt you
That's not how I want you to learn

With your kind heart
You might get burned
I hope that doesn't start
That's not what you earned

"Shining Through"

A spark
A word
A mark
Absurd

Do you see
What I feel
Can it be
Is this real

Words so pure
Time not wasted
Thoughts so sure
Actions hastened

Intentions well aimed
Often on the mark
Ambitions untamed
Escaped from the dark

"Birthday Gift"

I wish you joy
On your special day
You don't need money or toy
To help in this way

I don't mean to be sappy
But let the truth be known
Love can make you happy
You should never be alone

I offer a special gift
In this piece of art
Your spirits I hope to lift
This gift is my heart

I leave the rest up to you
It is for you to decide
I will understand whatever you do
As long as It comes from inside

I don't want to lose
The friendship we share
Whatever you choose
I know that you care

"Under Pressure"

One moves so near
The other moves away
Losing both I fear
Can't they both stay

I later find
This wish is twisted
The one following behind
Has now been black listed

She hangs with the wrong crowd
Rolls with the wrong crew
They make her loud
They cause trouble to brew

She'll be hurt
And left for dead
Or treated like dirt
For not using her head

That draws the line
He'll fall with a thud
Revenge will be mine
I will draw first blood

Second and last too
He has nowhere to run
There's no more to do
He's under the gun

"Loyalty and Sacrifice"

When you get right down to it
For you I'd give up my life
I have a sense of honor most can't fit
For you I'll face a knife

I'd take a shot
Right in the chest
When it gets hot
I'll take it so you can rest

I am very protective
Of those whom I love
Like a police detective
Or a winter glove

Attack my friend
You become my foe
Pity I do not lend
You're now on death row

When I strike
Fierce as a wild cat
You'll wish you took a hike
But you step up to bat

I attack with blind fury
I go straight for your head
You go down without glory
It's all over, you're dead

"Hidden Gems"

Gaze into the shadow
And see the purest light
Like peering thru a window
At a fire burning bright

The best things are well hidden
In unforgiving darkness
As if they are forbidden
A power all wish to harness

To obtain this great gift
Requires honor, love, and trust
To yield this power to lift
A pure heart is a must

A clouded mind will not do
It will only cause defeat
A clear and open point of view
Will push away deceit

Use it wisely
It will be true
Yield it falsely
It will destroy you

There is redemption
From this evil deed
Make no assumption
And you will succeed

"Blind Authority"

Mutiny comes to mind
When things are done his way
Knowing he is blind
It is like this each day

Creating great madness
To all those around
And a great sadness
As he runs them aground

To think just once
Would be a right step
Instead he is a dunce
With a hellish rep

He causes great turmoil
With his narrow-minded acts
He makes blood boil
By always changing the facts

He must always confuse
And no one understands
He feels its right to abuse
And refuse our demands

"Love Shines"

Love is a beautiful thing
As beautiful as a warm spring
Its strength surpasses wild imagination
It leads you to a wonderful destination

It brings happiness to your days
In many wonderful ways
It can make your days bright
It can make your heart light

"Overcast Lies"

The world is grey
The air is cold
The people say
Truth is dead or sold

It is not free
Which is not fair
There is a fee
For those who care

It relieves all fear
If not all the pain
It makes all clear
Even when in vain

To stop all the lies
And all the attacks
So all evil dies
We must tell only facts

"Mending"

I feel almost whole
I love the feeling
A mending soul
A steady healing

For the first time
A deep wonderful guy
That doesn't cost a dime
Going from a man back to a boy

Relaxed and carefree
Feeling like a person
Reborn strong for all to see
No longer coming undone

I spread my wings
I'm standing tall
Oh what strength freedom brings
I'm not afraid to fall

"Imploding World"

A world of joy
Shattered in no time flat
Broken like a child's toy
Knocked out cold on the mat

A heart crushed
A soul tortured and broken
Another dream flushed
Like an idle, worthless token

It's so hard to believe
That anyone cares
Their word deceives
But honesty no one dares

Swallowed by darkness
No happiness in sight
Can I become any less
Will I ever end the fight

I hope it is soon
Because I don't enjoy the pain
It's like staring at the moon
Thru an unforgiving rain

"Confusion and Disarray"

Does confusion rule your life
As it does mine
Does it cut like a knife
Yet cause pain no one sees

Does it hurt to think
Or make you zone out
Does it push you to the brink
For me there is no doubt

Do you like the way it feels
I can't say I do
Yet away the weakness peels
Making me strong and true

It can keep you bound
And also set you free
It makes your head pound
And never lets you be

It's not easy to handle
And it does abuse
Like turning a peaceful candle
Into a lit fuse

"Double Vision"

I begin to bleed
Seeing what I lost
It's a painful scene
For aside I've been tossed

I become confused
Now I see two
Yet others are amused
So evil yet so true

Must I choose
What I want for me
I will not abuse
The one it is to be

"Shedding Shadows"

My state is weak
The cut is deep
One to heal I seek
Until then I creep

In darkness I live
I search for the light
I don't think twice to give
I just feel it's right

As I look and look
Nothing do I find
My energy it took
I feel like I'm blind

What will it take to be glad
To turn it around and make good
To bring back the joy I had
To remove my black cape and hood

To shed this evil cloud
To go from loss to gain
With happiness endowed
To be out of the rain

I'm cut off from civilization
Alienated and alone
Not of my own creation
Isolated I've grown

"Withstanding Betrayal"

I've been stabbed in the back
With hope for my death
For survival I have a knack
I haven't taken my last breath

They hope I will fall
And be no more
Instead I stand tall
Not laid out on the floor

I may be cut
I may bleed
I may be hurt
They won't succeed

With all of my strength
I will look till I find
No matter the length
For someone to stand behind

"Seeking..."

My world is not whole
At this point in time
I have an empty soul
Isn't it a crime

It seems a shame
To feel like this
I wish it were in a frame
Turning into bliss

I look for the one and only
To find hope and pleasure
To end this feeling lonely
To gain someone to treasure

It may seem wrong
But I can't resist
I can't stay like this for long
This opportunity can't be missed

"Soothing Sounds"

All is silent
Yet peaceful, not
I know not my intent
I am not on the spot

Music keeps me calm
As does a voice
It leaves me with no qualms
Whose it is I have no choice

It opens my mind
And rests my soul
I can always find
Without taking its toll

It leads me to the right
Away from the wrong
It enhances my sight
It makes me strong

I move with ease
Thru space and time
Like a gentle breeze
With this music and rhyme

"Distance Closing"

I am so confused
I don't know what to do
I've been so abused
By all except you

You have always been here
To help me get by
You have always been near
When I was ready to cry

You show that you care
So the same I will try
To you my soul I will bare
And I will not pry

I am pushing many away
To you I wish not the same
I find pleasure every day
In hearing your name

"The Stand"

I lay down smooth rhymes
At the drop of a hat
Given a little time
I'll be at bat

You wanna keep it real
And face me toe-to-toe
If you can bring the real deal
Then back and forth we'll go

You can never win
With the shit you're packin'
To try is a sin
For which I'll be smackin'

You can walk away now
And get outta trouble
But if you don't bow
I'll bring it double

You're in too deep
Nowhere to run
My word I do keep
In the end you'll be done

"Mistakes"

I find no peace
As I am alone
It can only cease
If I atone

How can it be done
Who can help me thru
It won't be fun
If I find what to do

I wonder where to turn
Who to ask
Or should I just let it burn
As my own evil task

I look for a chance
To atone my mistakes
What is your stance
On how my soul breaks

"Anyone"

It really seems
No one gives a fuck
Everyone deems
It is just my luck

No one really knows
What it does to me
No one really shows
That they care or see

I hope this is not true
Although I cannot tell
I know no one's view
It makes me want to yell

I know not where to turn
I see no one there
It really leaves a burn
Too much for me to bare

If this is how you feel
Then turn and walk away
For this pain is real
I can't take it another day

"Fade"

The time has come
To face the end
I have fallen numb
Loss is the trend

No reason to continue
No need to go on
Only pain is in view
All happiness is gone

Wondering why
Pain falls on me
All good was a lie
Or can I not see

Do I go ahead
And seek pleasure
If this you have read
You have found my treasure

Or can I be saved
Will someone give aid
For now I'm enslaved
And away I slowly fade

"Hourglass"

Words from the heart
Hold more meaning
They are just a start
From what I'm seeing

It takes a little more
To find what you seek
Just open the door
If you're not too meek

Just make the first move
It may come to you
But if you find your groove
It's easier to do

You can't just sit by
And wait for things to come
Or away it may fly
And you will feel dumb

I know this first hand
I've watched the best pass
Thru my fingers like sand
Now I feel like an ass

IV
Discovery

"Steps and Growth"

A little skill
And a little luck
A little will
And a deal will be struck

Time will do its best
To accomplish its task
To surpass all the rest
And remove the mask

Shed the light on the truth
From the inside out
Although uncouth
Successful no doubt

To show all what is good
And what is so special
To remove the hood
And reveal the magical

As a phoenix from the ashes
A second coming of sorts
Making progress in dashes
Trying to steal a few hearts

Wishing for one
To give his own to
When all is said and done
He hopes it is you

"Weakness and Strength"

I don't have many weaknesses
Just maybe one or two
Most people think my meekness is
But this is far from true

To tell would be a mistake
A secret that could mean an end
A part of me some try to take
But the answer I do not lend

The one who knows
Knows not all the same
My weakness to them shows
As strength none could tame

"None" is not correct
As the number that could
Only one I detect
As someone who truly would

Weakness and strength
Are one in the same
To go to great length
It's all in a name

"Holding On"

Wish I could say
Wish I could do
Maybe one day
Till then I'll be blue

Time can fix the pain
If you sit back and relax
It can clear your brain
If you don't let it slip thru the cracks

You can stand tall
With the thought in your heart
No detail too small
If you're looking for a special part

Search long and hard
Look far and near
You don't want to be scarred
From losing something so dear

"Lingering Memories"

After I run my tongue and fingers
Over your body in bed
Your form still lingers
Forever in my head

I will never forget
The way I feel
And would only regret
If it was not real

I know it is real tough
From your look of enjoyment
I wish it were so
That this was my employment

You are my treasure
Which I did earn
I will give you true pleasure
When it is my turn

"Walking Away"

You made no wrong choice
In what you chose to do
You only used your voice
Based on what you knew

She didn't do the work
She needed to get by
You acted with an irk
And now you ask why

It was the only choice to make
To be just and fair
A lot of will it did take
So question don't you dare

"Rebuilding Dreams"

Shattered dreams
A broken heart
Never ending pain it seems
Will happiness ever start

Unless you find pleasure in pain
It's torture to the bone
It causes pure disdain
For those all alone

Hell could not compare
To what this can do
Attempt to endure if you dare
But it shall cripple or destroy you

Even the strongest fall to this power
The bravest quiver in fear
Even a hint of it could wilt a flower
And granite statues would shed a tear

You can't run
You can't hide
It can black out the sun
And reverse the tide

But to let it win
And push you under
Would be a sin
And a tremendous blunder

"Insanity"

Insanity rocks my being
Worry overwhelms me
All the things I'm seeing
How can this be

Buildings falling
Bridges burning
I hear a calling
I can't fight this yearning

Yet it is not to be mine
Never was never will
Yet I cannot resign
It is a battle uphill

I wish I could change
The ending I feel
The feeling isn't strange
It's a sensation all too real

"Broken"

An angel fallen
Unwanted and weak
Only to wonder when
It won't be so bleak

Trapped in a prison with no bars
No walls, barriers, or chains
Yet still kept from reaching the stars
As if someone else controls the reigns

Searching for freedom
And a release from this cell
For being in someone else's kingdom
Is truly pure hell

Shackled to the ground
Unable to fly
You hear the only sound
The tears of an angel's cry

Wings broken and battered
A heart is wounded and sore
Clothes torn and tattered
Patiently waiting for a cure

"The Final Battle"

I walk thru the fire
To face the devil
Like a mercenary for hire
To duel on another level

I pass thru the flame
Deeply burnt and scarred
No one to blame
My strength and will marred

A fight to the end
A challenge I partake
The honor I defend
This choice I make

A fierce fight ensues
Taking all of my power
My body he abuses
Yet I do not cower

Both fall to the ground
Lying in a pool of blood
Neither makes a sound
As we are spotted in mud

The end has come
But life is in the air
I move my arm some
Taking a breath as I stare

I rise to my feet
And see what I've done
My enemy I did defeat
My shadow over him in the sun

"Unbending"

Look at my face
And find something bleak
Look at my heart
And find something unique

Most don't look
To see that deep
What effort it took
What benefits it could reap

Yet no one wants to seek
To find what lies within
Not even to peek
Acting like it is a sin

Will it bring pain
Or true pleasure
Shelter from the rain
Is in this treasure

That no one yearns
To have as their own
Everyone turns
And I am alone

Yet I stand strong
And unbending brace
Under stress all day long
Yet of weakness there is no trace

Only one weakness
Is in the form of love
Possessing strength and callousness
Yet as gentle as a dove

With strong will
I fly thru the sky
Truly a thrill
To be up so high

"Reasons Change"

I'm torn apart
Left to die
Just to start
I know not why

Who will give
Who will care
Why do I live
Why do I share

Because I feel
Love that makes me strong
Is it real
Or am I wrong

I can only wonder
If it is true
Or is it my blunder
What will leave me blue

One thing alone
Keeps me in this world
This feeling I can't clone
Around it my fingers curled

No reason to go on
No reason to continue
Not all hope is gone
One steps into view

The only reason
For my life ongoing
Like a change in season
Or weather, raining to snowing

"Self-inflicted"

I drop to my knees
And look to the sky
I drown in the seas
Of the tears that I cry

Pain runs deep
Down to the bone
Sanity I cannot keep
In weakness I let out a moan

My armor they puncture
My blood slowly flows
I await the next juncture
When I shall return the blows

If I survive
To reach that point in time
I shall thrive
By using powerful rhyme

I stand above all
With this gift
Just one call
And my heart will not drift

It will tackle all fears
And conquer all who oppose
But you will see tears
That will give me strength I suppose

To fight any opponent
And come away with a win
Even with the component
I contain in sin

This sin is to care
For one I should not
One who is so fair
Yet it helps me a lot

Gives me strength
Gives me hope
I go to great length
To hold tight to the rope

"Fate's Reach"

I turn to one so fair
Who really doesn't know
How much I truly care
I'm not sure if I show

Words I hear for certain
Caused my mind to tailspin
Did I miss my curtain
Or did it never begin

Others just use me
Like some little toy
Is it fun to abuse me
Does it bring them joy

Yet I find one for whom I care
Who is just beyond my grasp
I know not if I should dare
To reach up and clasp

A treasure so dear
An angel on earth
Who makes all so clear
Who lifts me from the mirth

All seems dark
Save one point
Just a little spark
To this pain anoint

In cold I retreat
Trying to regroup
I don't accept it as defeat
Just re-arm the troop

But is it in vain
Or is there hope
Do I face the rain
Or stay against the rope

I hope I know soon
What I am to do
As I sit and look to the moon
I am writing this for you

"Misplaced Hope"

I turn to you
For strength and hope
I ask others what to do
They all say I must cope

I find strength in your sight
I feel healing in your touch
You make my spirit take flight
I wish to return feelings as such

As I see no chance
To bring happiness to thee
At least I got a chance
At absolute and pure glee

I don't easily give up
And I end up being smashed
Like an empty can or cup
My hopes and dreams are dashed

On the verge of tears
Holding in the pain
Not showing my fears
This attempt made in vain

I question all my motives
Is there a point to holding back
Or should I light up the votives
Discretion should I lack

I fear I will lose
Everything we possess
I don't want to choose
I can't take the stress

My head pounds
My heart is ready to burst
As strange as it sounds
I feel as if I'm cursed

There is no way to tell
What it will take
To see who cast this spell
And what will cause it to break

"Knightly Devotion"

I owe you my existence
Yet you have no clue
There is still a great distance
And for this I am blue

I owe you everything
All your hopes and dreams
For the happiness you bring
I can't give you enough it seems

And yet I need not give
That is for the other
Yet I'd give up the life I live
For the joy of another

No matter when you miss
I put your happiness first
If you experience bliss
I can live on being cursed

I bow to you Milady
For you I do adore
If you feel my motives shady
Feel free to deeply explore

I am true to my word
As you are happy, so am I
Don't think it absurd
When you see me fly

Fly to new heights
Or to your side
Your happiness in my sights
Your rules I abide

This knight drops to one knee
A humble servant of his queen
Knowing her love is not for he
Risking life and limb to keep a peace that has been

"Friends"

I open the door
I see pure hell
My knees hit the floor
Who can I tell

I drop to my knees
Most run away
No one truly sees
Yet I do not stray

I see few by my side
Yet they lift me from distress
They help me not hide
It is done to help, not impress

They give me a hand
To get to my feet
They are steady land
They shield me from the heat

Most turn their back
But all do not
Those that do, lack
Loyalty when on the spot

Loyalty and honor
The mark of true friends
Not to turn on him or her
Here evil begins and friendship ends

I leave all behind
Those I cannot trust
To help clear my mind
Find friendship or bust

"Tangible Mirage"

I feel a gentle breeze
Pushing an aroma thru the air
Light reflects a mirage on the seas
Only an angel could be so pretty, so fair

Intoxicated by the sight
My mind wanders
No urge to fight
The ideas my soul ponders

A peace is felt
A calmness settles in
All pain begins to melt
As if it had never been

It was a tough struggle
Fighting for every bit
Even though there was much to juggle
It all seems worth it

"Mask"

Not allowed to stand tall
Obstacles at every turn
No respect from family at all
Anger starts to burn

Being torn at the seams
Pulled apart inside and out
The attacks are in teams
Raising too much doubt

Since when do I deserve torment
I have done no wrong
I get nothing but discontent
It's getting hard to stand strong

They all preach respect
Yet give none for what they ask
Hypocritical I detect
So I don't put on that mask

"Treasure Trove"

A wonderful treasure
I found in this sweet lady
Being near her is a pleasure
Is it possible, or am I crazy

Her eyes a beautiful blue
Her hair a golden blonde
As if from a special brew
Or touched by a magic wand

She changes boredom to fun
Turns sadness into joy
Destroys darkness like the sun
Makes everything easier to enjoy

"Love is"

Love is hope
It does not die
All at once it's a binding rope
And the ability to fly

I cannot change
The love I feel
I wouldn't want to exchange
And it's not a wound to heal

It is for you always
You have held it true
I cherished it all of these days
It amazed me how it grew

And still it grows
With every passing moment
It emanates and grows
Never feeling like an opponent

You made a decision
Of which you said you're sure
It isn't what we envision
But it is completely pure

Your happiness is what I crave
To see you smile and laugh
I hope you see this in how I behave
Though, of what I would do, this is not half

"Drifting..."

We drift slowly apart
Or so it seems
It pains my heart
Simply consequence everyone deems

I wish not to lose you
I wish it were different
But this much is still true
To my angel I give commitment

No matter where you go
No matter how far apart we drift
I just want you to know
Your love is a wonderful gift

The tear in my eye
Shows how I feel
I try not to cry
As I now must deal

"Vision of Joy"

Have you ever had a feeling
You didn't want to let go
Felt like you're walking on the ceiling
Never wanting to say no

Has a hug meant the world
Brought time to a standstill
Like a tornado twirled
Made the whole experience a thrill

It's a feeling of joy
A sensation unmatchable
Not being a toy
Is something remarkable

"Lies and Deceit"

Time crawls by
Life moves on
No point to ask why
You know any answer is a con

No one can be honest
Even to save themselves
To this I can attest
As deeper the devil delves

The truth is never known
As if it were wrong
Away I am blown
That lies can grow for so long

So many lies
So many people deceived
Any truth someone tries
Can never be believed

"Unheard Cries"

The fire burns
The anger grows
My stomach turns
The aggression flows

Violence is warranted
But allowed not
Important things taken for granted
Lost in the crowd

A pain is caused
That should not be
It appears time has paused
To allow all to see

A dark cloud
Looms over head
The brooding storm very loud
Yet everything seems dead

A sign of extreme trouble
An unforeseen fear
That could easily double
From cries we do not hear

"Humbly Righteous"

Walking thru the shadows
Alone from the start
The only way he knows
Walking with an empty heart

No one really cares
People just pass him by
Someone stops and stares
So he turns to ask them why

They turn away and scurry off
Like an evil demon did speak
Or a diseased man did cough
It is like that every day of the week

But when someone's in need
He'll help without hesitation
He'll do most any deed
He'll go to most any destination

Although it goes unnoticed
He doesn't do it for attention
For his deeds are always dismissed
Like there is no need for mention

He acts as he feels right
Actions he feels are just
He uses all his might
Because he feels he must

"Alone I Break"

If I were to disappear
It wouldn't matter much, would it
I'd realize my one fear
No one would miss me a bit

I'm not good enough for most
I can't meet anyone's standard
I'm not worth anyone's boast
It always has to be so hard

Needs can always be met
Whether I'm here or not
I'm willing to bet
Most can fill my spot

I'm losing those most dear
Even though some have no clue
And yet no one can hear
What makes me so blue

"This Is Equality?"

I'm expected to be better
Than everyone around
Follow the rules to the letter
I'm being driven into the ground

I am supposed to do more
While everyone else does much less
Like I'm living up to some kind of lore
And it's just becoming a large mess

Making life harder on everyone
Causing conflicts to arise
Weighing everyone down a ton
Making it easier no one tries

It's left for me to do
Solely my responsibility
And for all I've done for you
You're losing respectability

"Inner Fire"

I sit up at night
Staring at the wall
Wondering if you're alright
Waiting patiently for your call

For you to be ok
Is all I ever desire
At night or during the day
Feels like a blazing fire

Tears I shed
That no one sees
The fire's fed
It lives and breathes

You deserve the best
And nothing less
You're above the rest
You should have pure happiness

It burns of love
For one so dear
Like the song of a dove
I wish you could hear

"Merry Christmas"

The snow falling outside
The fire burning bright
Sleigh awaiting our ride
It's a beautiful sight.

The tree in the den
Covered in lights
Everyone wondering when
They can sample the sweet delights

Presents under the tree
Stockings stuffed to the brim
Enough so all can see
What you got for him

It's not how much you spent
He shouldn't really care
It's about the love you sent
And all the feelings you share

No matter how commercial it gets
There's always something more
The season always lets
Us share something pure

So break out the mistletoe
Pour some eggnog
Cuddle up for the show
Of the burning Yule log

For it's not the presents
Or the lights
Or the meals
Or the shows

It's the commitments
And delights
Everyone feels
And bestows

Merry Christmas

"Peaceful Rest"

The rain falls outside
The wind blows gently through
My mind takes a magical ride
Among wonderful thoughts of you

You have a touch
No one can match
You can share so much
And I never feel there's a catch

You bring a smile to my face
You open my eyes
Sadness disappears without a trace
You clear the darkest skies

I drift to a far off land
Music plays and the stars dance
The rain is soft like the touch of your hand
Causing me to yearn for a glance

The wind whispers your name
It is carried far and wide
I've never heard anything so tame
That can turn all pain aside

"Future"

The future is cloudy
No one knows what lies there
We move forward not giving it a thought
Then someone comes along
Making us want to know what it holds
And makes us fear it at the same time

The fear doesn't stop you
It guides you toward that someone
It takes a back seat to a feeling
So amazing and strong
That the fear vanishes for moments

It brings about a yearning
A longing
For that which you fear
It gives a sensation
That what you fear is worth the chance

"Hard Path"

I don't always know the right words
Or the right steps to take
But I only wish the best
To help, calm, and cheer

You hold my heart
It's in your hands
When you're sad it wants
To hug away your tears

When you're afraid it yearns
To hold you and tell you it'll be ok
When things look dark
Its love burns to light your way

Time alone is something
We all need from time to time
But not all steps need
To be taken alone

Sometimes we don't need
A guide or an ear
Sometimes we just need
A hand to hold tight
Just to know someone is there
And we're not walking down
The hard path alone

"Life's Cell"

You're amazing, the best I've ever seen
You're one of a kind, almost perfect
These words are sharp and keen
But you must have a defect

There's always someone better
Someone who is everything you're not
Marked with some kind of letter
Or cursed to be a part of the lot

But just maybe it's not you that's flawed
Maybe it's those looking upon you
Who, at your flesh, have clawed
And Stabbed at your heart too

Maybe they feed you lies
Give you false sights and hopes
Like they yearn for your cries
And try to bind you with these ropes

These ropes that tie your hands
Bind them together behind
Mark you with their brands
Trapping you in your own mind

Before you give in to your own deception
Take a good look inside your heart
There is more there than just redemption
There is what will make their lies depart

The original words they spoke are true
You are the person they described so well
It shows they had more than a clue
And wanted to trap you in their cell

"Breaking Down Walls"

You build up a wall
As it grows higher
You hear a call
It feels like a fire

A hole appears
Burned slowly thru
Should it strengthen your fears
Or bring peace to you

You feel a little of both
More peace than uncertainty
Words coming like an oath
Or a familiar litany

An arm reaches in
The wall starts to crumble
But if you let it begin
Can you stop the tumble

To enclose another
Is an impossible feat
You can't contain or cover
Anyone else's heat

Vulnerable and open
Just another test
No idea what will happen
But it will pass like the rest

"Stronger"

Sleep escapes me
Thoughts spin wildly
Thru the darkness
They fly ferociously
Colliding thunderously

Nothing new
Nothing surprising
But still just as frightening
Still as unnerving

A test of desire maybe
Or a challenge of spirit
A swipe at faith
A battle of strength

The blows strike with fury
I come close to losing my balance
Staggering just a little
Not wavering or falling

The greater the goal
The harder the path
The more you work
The stronger you become

"Smoke and Mirrors"

Things look one way
But are much different
There is a thick shade of grey
Making the close feel so distant

Hiding the truth from sight
Distorted reflections are cast
Darkness choking the light
Images changing so fast

Clouded and choking
Constricting movement
Surroundings smoking
Not exposing its intent

Burns your eyes
Dries your throat
Tells you lies
Covering your mind in another coat

Coat of distrust
Wounds deep but unseen
Lying in a cloud of dust
Looking quite green

Truths coated in lies
Facts no one hears
No one heeds your cries
In a world of smoke and mirrors

"Bad Day?"

Ever have a day
That passed too slowly
A day you wish you could do over
Or forget all together

But when all was said and done
You enjoyed it
More so than you thought possible

You limp thru the day
In a haze, on autopilot
The minutes tick away
Anticipating the final bell

You expect no less
Than what you felt all day
What should be different now

But something has changed
Something's gone wrong
More precisely, gone right
A change in the wind
A clearing in the sky

You walk out the door
Under the setting sun
And it all melts away

Your shoulders relax
Tension drifts away
Things brighten and clear
A smile creeps across your face
A bad day made great

"Lakeside Evening"

A quiet night
Stars filling the sky
Such a beautiful sight
Watching the clouds drift by

A gentle breeze
Carries through the air
The bounty of leaves
Attracting your stare

You sit on the dock
The stars dance on the lake
The darkness they mock
As your attention they take

A ripple flows
Fireflies give chase
A warm smile grows
Across your moonlit face

A boat drifts along
The trees are dancing
The crickets play their song
One beautiful lakeside evening

"Blindness"

Blindness abounds
People see what they want
Missing the most obvious of things

How much can you listen
The more words spoken
The clearer it becomes

Actions went unnoticed
What you gave had no value
What was it worth
What was the point

Who cares
Why do
Who knows
Why try
Who asks
Why bother
Who sees
Why believe

V
New Beginnings

"Darkness"

Darkness drifts in
Fog coats the ground
Something evil fills the air
Nightmares become real

Off in the shadows
An outline appears
Faint and unmoving
Almost non-existent

A faint purple glow appears
From the eyes of the outline
Becoming only a little clearer
But that much more real

Lightning flashes
Framing a pale face
For only a second
Giving only a glimpse

A glimpse of eternity
A moment of evil
A second of peace
A future of torment

Blood drips from the corners
Of his pale lips
His eyes solid red
His fangs sharp as daggers

In a flash
He is gone
Leaving you empty
In more ways than one

"Winter Wonderland"

Soft snow falls
Lightning flashes
Yet no thunder is heard

No longer bitter cold
But wrapped in a blanket of warmth

Taken back to days past
Of winter frolic
Beautiful coated trees
Quiet streets and peaceful hills

A walk down thru the park
A snowball fight in the street
Hot cocoa with friends

A couple by the fire
Sharing the warmth
Sharing each other
The joy of a winter wonderland

"Peace"

Things change so fast
Day to day almost nothing is the same
Weather is unpredictable
Human nature holds no guarantees
Snow falls one day
And melts away the next
Life is in disarray

Amongst the chaos
A smile shines through
To bring peace to your heart
From an endearing soul

In Loving Memory of Kim Belly

"Ice Drake"

Darkness rolls in
Across fields of soft white
The temperature falls
Time appears to stand still

He emerges from his cave
His blue scales shimmering
Beneath the moonlight
Stretching and yawning
Awakening from his slumber

His burning red eyes
Scanning the landscape
Taking a deep breath
Chest filling with brisk winter air

He grins warmly
Spreads his wings
And with a great leap
The Ice Drake takes flight

"Survival"

Standing tall
Upon a boulder
Covered by the falling snow
Eyes narrowed
Mouth dripping
Staining the snow

Perched over his fallen prey
Blood dripping slowly
His beautiful white coat marred
The dark stripes masking only some
The peace broken by the need for survival

"Calm"

A Fire burns
Light dancing on the trees
Stars glimmer above

Wood crackling
Occasional howls and hoots
Fireflies fading in and out
Bats flying overhead

A beautiful spring evening
Not a cloud in the sky
Wolf cubs playing games
Darting thru the wild
Leaving the muted calm of the wild

"Ecstasy"

Music softly playing in the background
She looks into his eyes
Searching deeply for the answer
Asking: "Do you want me?"

A quiver in her lip
A yearning in her eyes
Her hand in his

He returns her gaze
Answering her with a softness
That falls over his face
With a deep kiss
And a passionate embrace

Followed by a soft caress
Tracing her curves
First by fingers
Then by lips and tongue
Enjoying her entirety
Entwined in each other
Becoming one with the moment

Minutes tick away
Becoming hours
Though time appears to stand still
Nothing else matters
Just the two of them
The world melts away
Leaving an aura of ecstasy

"Eternal Darkness"

Lightning crashes
A flash uncovers
The shady character
Slowly walking

His skin pale
Eyes a deep red
Long, sharp nails
Tussled hair

Welcome to my world
Welcome to my darkness
His words chilling
His gaze unnerving

Left feeling weak
Life dripping down your chest
The world begins to spin
Heart racing

Suddenly peace
The world appears most beauteous
Every sound music to your ears
The world is yours

The cool breeze calms
The fresh air awakens
You are one with the night
At peace in eternal darkness

"Tears from Heaven"

Clouds thicken
The sky darkens
A chill fills the air
A somber scene unfolds

Harsh times are coming
Evil grows strong
Great loves are lost
Joy seems to disappear

Rain starts to fall
Moods change quickly
Angels begin to cry
Shedding tears from heaven

"Trapped"

Trapped in your own mind
Like a cell or blocked cave
Not knowing your place
Sure to unsure in the blink of an eye
Longing for some sense of self

Wandering through the day
Blinded by the simplest of things
Lost in confusion
Searching for a door

A fog hides the path
Rolling silently in
The air is getting thick
You struggle to breathe
Hearing a voice say "Don't Fight"
You close your eyes
And suddenly you're gone

"Technology"

So dependent on technology
So attached to the internet
Blind to the joys surrounding you

The cool night air
A loving pet
A soft glowing candle
Music dancing quietly to your ears

A soft sigh
A warm smile
A feeling of peace
Flowing over you

Stepping into your moment
You pick up your pencil and pad
And let your magic flow

"Father Time"

Tired eyes
A weary heart
Days grow longer
Hours pass like seconds
Time fades in a flash
But no progress is seen

Years vanish
And we wonder where to go
Just yesterday was January
But it's already July
Soon December will be here
And the year will draw to a close

Bones grow weak
Our light begins to fade
Father Time takes our hand
Leading us to our destination
Laying us to eternal rest

"Believe"

From a young age
Something guides us
Draws us forward
Takes our hand
Shows us where to go

As we grow
We're taught about
What should and shouldn't be
Groomed to resist ourselves
Fight what leads us

This task is difficult at first
But as we're taught
The struggle lessens
Facts cloud feelings
Instinct becomes intellect
Part of us fades
If it can't be proven
It can't be true

We become slaves to "fact"
Learning more and more
Losing touch with what we truly believe

"Virgin Soul"

Life brought into the world
Innocent and new
Expecting nothing
Knowing less
Into a new family

Only love should they show
But anger and mistrust prevail
Lost in the fray
Blind to the joys of life
Hurting silently

Not able to express
What she feels inside
Not yet able to speak
Unsure if she could
That it would make a difference

Parents oblivious to their effect
On a virgin soul
Not seeing past their nose
Single-minded and uncompromising
Fighting at every turn

She fights to free her soul
Spread her wings and fly
Share her joy and love
Without saying a word
Wondering if she will make a difference

"Truth"

Quiet shadows trailing behind
Concealing words and feelings
Hiding the truth but also the lies
Casting an air of confusion
Whispers pulling in all directions
No hint of their origins

Distant mumbles drift around corners
Footsteps grow eerily closer
Then silence returns
A faint flicker brings a small glimmer of hope
Quashed in an instant by an imposing outline
Monstrous and frightening

Moving closer, filling the passageway
With a wave of its hand
Speaking a solitary word
The shadows vanish as quickly as they appeared
Truth clears your mind
Leaving a smile and feeling of peace

Fear and confusion dissipate
Walking along with head held high
The future has a new clarity
You never thought possible

"One Day"

I closed my eyes
Slowly exhale
Fighting the lies
Chasing my tail

Watching the torment
Someone close trapped
My anger grew
My feelings uncapped

But back in she walks
To uncaring arms
Despite how she talks
Or how bad he harms

She speaks of discontent
Of the need to escape
Of a lack of commitment
Of her life's odd shape

Yet no action taken
No attempts made
Her confidence shaken
Her heart so afraid

He's ruined her spirit
Destroyed her will
He treats her like shit
He feels it's a thrill

One day she'll see
Hopefully not too late
Where she should be
Is with someone great

"...The Stars"

Castles and horses
Knights and ladies
Honor has meaning
Justice is raw
Competition is fierce
Friendship is true

Swords and shields
Kings and queens
Pride is blinding
Greed is poisoning
The sun warms our days
And our hearts guide our path

The future isn't written in stone
Each of us can change our stars

VI
Lessons Learned

"Love's Insight"

The longer I listen
The less I say

The less I say
The more I'm thinking

The more awkward I act
The more I want to impress

The harder I try
The more I care

The more I write
The deeper I feel

The deeper I feel
The quieter I get

I'm left at a loss
Not knowing what to say
Not wanting to screw up
And look like a fool

And yet the harder I try not to
The funnier and more foolish I become
The quieter I get
The farther I drift

Walking the winding path
Confused and yet seeing clearly
Not knowing which fork to take
But knowing I can't stay here

One path straight and unobstructed
The other winding and rocky
I want the wide and free path
But the best goals are hard to achieve

Delays seem inevitable
But what is the cost
What do I lose while I wait
What will pass me by

It's time to move forward
Down a long and difficult road
One foot in front of the other
One step at a time

I know what I must do
And what I'll face along the way
Challenges I've never faced before
Weights I couldn't fathom carrying

There will be some bumps along the way
A few tears and maybe some blood
But I've made my choice
And I'll see it to the end

"Losing Humanity"

I find myself yearning
For a time gone by
When life was simple
And people cared about each other

A time before avarice ruled the world
Before politically correct existed
When speech was truly free
And the word offensive had meaning

A time without fear of telling a child no
Or letting them play outside
When it was safe to climb trees
And drink water from the garden hose

I find myself yearning
For a time gone by
When life was simple
And people cared about each other

A time when respect was earned
Not demanded based on age or income
When trust and honesty were welcomed
While deceit and corruption were protested

A time before mistrust consumed society
Before darkness seemed all encompassing
When crime was punished unequivocally
And the innocent weren't treated so heinously

I find myself yearning
For a time gone by
When life was simple
And people cared about each other

A place where nature was appreciated
Not buried under developmental destruction
When trees and lakes weren't uprooted and filled in
In the name of ingenuity and progression

A time when people wed for love
Not for the needed income and support
When mistakes were learned from
Not dismissed to be repeated time and again

I find myself yearning
For a time gone by
When life was simple
And people cared about each other

A time when a person was judged on character
Instead of the size of their exuberant possessions
When life's struggles were learning experiences
Not an insurmountable mountain of distress

A time when people were people
Not just working class slaves
When violence was considered a last resort
Not the one and only solution

I find myself yearning
For a time gone by
When life was simple
And people cared about each other

A time when smiles were shared
And hugs were cherished gifts
When the future seemed bright
And we were far from losing humanity

"To Be A Man"

What does it mean
"To be a Man"
How best to learn
Is to figure out what it doesn't.

Does it mean having the biggest muscles?
No.
Does it mean being the biggest dick?
No.
Does it mean being able to beat your girlfriend?
No.
Does it mean being able to push people around?
No.
Does it mean having the most money?
No.
Does it mean thinking you're better than everyone else?
No.
Does it mean making things around you the way you want them?
No.

What does it mean?

Having the intelligence to walk away,
Having the heart to help and protect those who need it.
Giving everything you have, despite of what you want.
Having the strength to not assault those weaker than you,
Knowing you're better than those who think they're the world.
Yet knowing you're no better than the woman standing next to you.
Having the ability to change yourself to make the world around you
better,
Knowing that compassion can be just as important as punishment,
Seeing that being able to help someone is more important than
being able to hurt them.
Having the soul to feel that controlling someone else is impossible.
Yet controlling ourselves is vital.

That is what it means,
"To be a man"

"I want to write..."

I want to write words
That will tie your mind in knots
And make your heart skip a beat

I want to form lyrics
That catch your ear
And make you move your feet

I want to create a story
That brings you to tears
But makes you cheer at the end

I want to weave a tale
That will trap you in its lines
Like you've been placed under a spell

I want to make you feel comfortable
Like you're sitting at home
In a place you can't see or touch

I want to open the door
To a place you thought
Could never exist

I want to put into words
All the things people wanted to say
But didn't have the courage

I want to write...

"Our Guardian Angels"

Standing silently, fighting bravely
Brave men and women of our Armed Forces
Giving everything they have
Expecting nothing in return

Helmet on her head
Rifle on his shoulder
Boots on his feet
Honor in her heart

Hearing the call of duty
Answering the bell without a thought
Facing dangers day and night
Eating little and sleeping less

Protecting our lives
Keeping us safe
At the cost of life and limb
Ceaselessly defending God and Country

His faith is interminable
Her spirit indomitable
His soul pure and strong
Her head held high

She spreads her wings
Shielding us from the fire
He shines his light
Guiding us to safety

Our Guardian Angels
Protectors and defenders
Giving everything they have
Expecting nothing in return

"Truest Freedom"

An angel in chains
Trapped inside walls
Made by political games
And legal mumbo jumbo

A soul meant to be free
To soar through the clouds
Gliding above the waves
Drops glistening in the sun

Eyes shining brighter
Than the stars above
Her heart as pure
As the freshly fallen snow

Despite her chains
She finds the truest freedom
In the words in her heart
And the voice of her little Angel

"Poetry is..."

Poetry is...

Poetry is a glimpse at the soul
A window to the heart
A whisper in a noisy room
A comforting touch during frightening times

Poetry is a new light in the darkness
New eyes to see the world
New ears to follow the music
New hands to hold tight the reigns of life

Poetry is a respite from sorrow
A cessation of pain
A realization of potential
An emancipation of confusion

Poetry is a new strength in times of despair
A renewed hope for brighter days
A new vigor for adventures
A renewed passion for life and love

Poetry is the cry of a newborn baby
The first steps of a toddler
The smile of a new bride and groom
The last steps of a cherished grandparent

Poetry is words on a page
A picture in a frame
A tree in the fall
The stars in the sky

Poetry is what you take from it
What you put into it
What you see in it
What you hear from it

Poetry is growth
Poetry is fantasy
Poetry is reality
Poetry is truth
Poetry is hope

Poetry is love
Poetry is joy
Poetry is life
Poetry is everything

Poetry is...

"Enchanted Emerald"

A starry twinkle in her eye
A warming smile on her face
A soul unclouded as a dove
And a heart of pure gold

Imparted with a magick
Enchanting and majestic
Lucky few will ever behold
And still fewer ever obtain

Nothing regular about her
Yet just the girl next door
Someone you could see every day
And still have to look twice

An imagination untamed
Yet so down to earth
Caring and dedicated
Yet tempestuous and unconstrained

Strong and determined
Yet tender and forgiving
She can liberate your heart
And unmask your soul

Catch her if you can
But be ready to set her free
When she spreads her wings
She cannot be restrained

"Choices"

Halo teetering precariously
On mystically pointed and anointed horns
Leathery wings cast looming shadows
Over a glowing angelic form

Kneeling on the cold stone
Feeling the heat emanate from below
A battle of wills, a locking of horns
Indecision and confusion

Invisible strings pulling us
Tugging our soul in different directions
Attempting to guide us both ways at once
Forcing us to choose for ourselves

Willing ourselves to make a declaration
Show the world our tenacity and resolve
Molding our mind and distinguishing our soul
Procuring our virtues and unearthing ourselves

Standing tall with newly endowed strength
Breaking the imperceptible bonds
Swelling to exceed our potential
Realizing we are finally free

"Passion..."

Passion...

The deep burning
Yearning and profound desire
To take part in something
That makes us whole

Passion...

The fire that grows
With every soft kiss
Entwining touch and lingering gaze
From the one we hold so dear

Passion...

The undeniable sensation
That you belong
In a precise location
Whether in a book or on the sand

Passion...

The interminable allure
Of the music of life
From the beat of a heart
To raindrops on a pane of glass

Passion...

The ceaseless gratification
Of an impeccably tuned and polished car
Roaring fiercely down the road
Glistening curves kissed gently by the sun

Passion...

The sudden spark
That makes us fight
Like a wildcat backed into a corner
For who we are and what we believe in

Passion...

The instinct we heed
To challenge our limits
Breaking our boundaries
For the truth of our virtues

"Unfinished"

Words on a faded page
Ideas hanging on the wind
Teasing hearts and minds
Flirting with open souls

Words from the heart
Never finding the lips
Like the melody of life
Drifting away on the wind

The "I'm Sorry" we feel
But never get to say
The "I love you" we need
But never manage to share

The dance we craved
But were afraid to ask for
The song we wished to sing
But were too shy to share the tune

The day at the park
Passed for a day at the computer
The game of catch with friends
Neglected in search of advancement

Words on a faded page
Ideas hanging on the wind
Thoughts and actions left
Parts of a life unfinished...

www.ingramcontent.com/pod-product-compliance
Lightning Source LLC
Chambersburg PA
CBHW020514100426
42813CB00030B/3246/J